2005 BO

CW00481114

CHRISTOPHER SANDERSON
A COASTMOOR PUBLICATION

ISBN:9798612579779

...in silence that is only there
when trust and hope are weak

START AGAIN: LIFE'S ITINERANT CHOICES

Foreword

I had to go, I felt I had no choice; if I was to stay where would I lay my voice; too close would not unleash the pain, too far would in time deliver its own tarnished stain.

My most difficult year to date, mentally, physically, psychologically; I was suffering the heartache and torment of a failed relationship.

These are the poems of that year, offered in chronological order, there are two volumes such that the weight which I offload does not weigh you down.

This work is part of a long term retrospective, there are, and have been minor edits along the way but hopefully the tangled mind shows through the disentanglements.

Poetry was partly responsible for the break-up, but also responsible for the getting together in the first place seventeen years before.

Now poetry became the salvation, a place to tempt my weary soul to say what needed to be said in an attempt to keep my mind, my body, and my soul looking ever forwards.

Enjoy

Christopher

February 2020

THE POEMS: LIFE'S ITINERANT LOSS

The Waves Roll Over And Over

The waves roll over and over
Rolling across the curve of the shoreline
Their stereophonic splashes wash over, wash over

Silently the sodium lights glaze the ripples
Incidentally highlighting the ebb, the flow
All the while buoys and marker lights bobble, flicker

Seen through the open, broken bathroom door
This after Yentob on Freud, on the radio
Only pretending to understand

Wanting to remember this time
Wanting to describe the space
Describe the feeling

Sodium at the seafront
At midnight
No other sounds

Sea moving, salt-air flowing
Earlier, Hockney saying that painting
Painting is the real thing

A photograph could not capture the scene
You know what, he is almost right
But behind me is the sink

Down below the window
A solitary moment, a stranger passing
Neither captured, by flashbulb, nor by paintbrush

Both unable to synthesise all of the view
But with these thought out words
Written down, beside the corroded

Glass cracked single glazed window
With a cream windowsill on the inside
Outside a sky-blue, mottled, blemished paint

I can look out into the blackness
Describe that now there is no horizon
Only a two-dimensional black space

A completely starless night sky
How would the painter work?
Without depth or perspective

How would the photographer touch?
The thousand miles of nothingness
Between here and the next continent

Or remember the background sounds
Beach-bound pebbles crashing
Like a sack of marbles

Or the roar
Of the last motorbike
As he serenades

Then leaves
The shoreline esplanade
Maybe it is for the last time

Poets, Tarts, Pimps and Writers

Black stockings, spotted skirt
Engaging smile, pretty flirt, dealing dirt
Dollars or dope, just enough rope

Bring her home, she's never alone
Violence in love, her presence she moves
The crescent moon, it cannot rise too soon

Black in black, coffee cafe, jukebox jive
He's so alive it's killing him
His girl works, he shows her the door

He has to score, it's killing him
Shining silver, leaves of gold
Everything he holds, he has sold for his soul

She is escaping from within, mescaline frightens
Her skin, her nerves, pray to quieten
Stronger, the fool took her time

Nearly took her total, she longs to be strong again
Singing songs, clean and confident, sort of freedom
Yet still on the edge

A need to perform, limited by reform
Don't want to get at it again
He's doing time, paying his fine, corrupting society

Importing exploitation, prostituting the situation
In a year, she's still clear, but now he's out
He's roundabout, no change, still the strange

Satisfaction of manipulation

Of course she falls, no one to call, he holds her tight

Says it's all right; he cares, he smiles, he stares

Fear or love, god above, god only knows

Having been before, why the need to score

Why go on the game again

A passion for crime, even doing time

Learning new tricks, corrupting young hicks

Building reputations, avoiding situations-vacant

The new black economy

Talk about arts, sculptors, fighters

About poets, tarts, pimps and writers

Welcome, To The South Shore

Welcome
Welcome to the South Shore
Welcome
Welcome to the Promenade

Won't you, won't you kiss me quickly
Won't you, wont you kiss me hard

Jo and Tan
Holding hands
They never can
When staying home

Welcome
Welcome to the South Shore
Welcome to the Promenade
Kiss me
Kiss me

Jo and Tan
Need your love
Trying hard
To understand

Joe and Tan
Come to terms
Society expands
Culture blinds, culture burns

Welcome
Welcome to the South Shore
Welcome to the Promenade

Kiss me
Kiss me quickly
Kiss me slow

Jo and Tan
Tiptoes of expectation
Love is no surprise
Summits of sensation

Joe and Tan
Wrapped in exultation
Inside each others skin
Breathing breath together

Welcome
Welcome to the South Shore
Welcome to the Promenade
Kiss me
Kiss me more

Joe and Tan
Candy floss
Piers for souvenirs
Take me home

Joe and Tan
Break down
The treasonable pretences
Shake us to our senses

Joe and Tan
Boy and Girl
Save the world
Live your life of love

Welcome
Welcome to the South Shore
Welcome
Welcome to the Promenade

Won't you
Won't you love me, slowly
Wont you, wont you
Won't you love me anyhow

Invitation

Where are you now
Write to me more often
Where are we now
Softly spoken

Where I am
Fairly softened
There you are then
Nothings broken

Writing invitations
Simulating sensations
The coffee's safe
In Massarella's café

The light is dense
Behind the lens
I smile awhile
In a magic-moment style

Where are you now
Write to me more often
Where are we now
Excited slowly spoken

Knocks on the head
Some say still I suffer
Knocks on the head
Woken, woken to usher

Concentrate, imagine
A transparent minds ride

Postulate, bring to life's design
Disordered thoughts reside

Motivate
Drive me madly
Introvert
Take me gladly

Where are you know
Write to me more often
Where I am now
Panicking, stupendously

A birth is more special
Than I can contemplate
A life is more special
Than I cared to situate

How to release
Unwise ineffectual pressures
But retain, explain the disease
Love, compassion, mindful seizures

Where are you now
Write to me more often
Grow me, overtly
Covet me, sensually

I feel to exude
High expectation
Is this received
Perceived, or an untrue situation

You seem able

Stable, of invention
Thoughtful, real, capable
Is it true of you; you of abstention

Supportive, or disruptive
Challenging or cajoling
Balancing or instructive
I, or you, or our bias rolling

Energy flows
The picture grows
The smiles return
Doubts they do still burn

Where are you now
Speak to me
Speak to me more often
Kick me

Metaphorically
Engage me
Excessively, seriously
Draw me, repeatedly

Tell me
What I should give too
Pray, demand of me
To reach, reach within you

Command, perhaps with dander
On reflection
The growth should meander
A little closer to perfection

Where are you now
Still with me
With me so more often
Being somehow

Distraction
Extracting self satisfaction
Self sufficient
Unaware of layered intent

People need people
Communication connects consumption
Interaction is as a steeple
The second oxygen of life, of gumption

Where are you now
Will you; wow
Will you see
One day I, I becoming we, more often

I Pretty Much Trust Magnetism

Of people, of ideas, of jewels
Of music, of prayers, of laughs
Of drugs, of glances, of guilt
Of fire, of water, of storms
Of, you know, those
Naturally occurring pulls toward
I'd go further than that in fact
That trust, that magnetism
People swaying, ideas playing
Clusters of jewels, mountains of music
Mosques, synagogues, chapels, churches
Prayer, laughter - those hugs of civilisation
No longer scared of sideways glances
No more guilt to be bound
Neither from the fire, nor from the water
Instead to embrace the reviving storms

You Are A Long Way From Home

It seems to me
From the way you dress
That you are a long way
A long way from home

I also surmise, surprise
That you are lost
Lost inside, I find
Inside your sketchbook world

Looking backwards
Back along the promenade
To the turret, to the tower
They are your silhouettes

The clock in the square
The coronation cross
They are your foreground
Your definition, your detail

This picture
Framed to the East
Framed by the faraway shores
Beyond the distance, beyond the horizon

These Jurassic cliffs crumble
Their history cloaks another mankind
You are I surmise
A long way from home

Are you here to escape
Escaping the troubles of mad mankind

Are you here, stored away, but crippled
Crippled, by your wandering mind

The stillness, the calm
Of this present situation
Behind the wars, behind the warriors
Is it they that test your patience

The injustice of your situation
Not by choice, or in context
Simply an artist drawing
On what's left of this day's life

The light is fading
You have moved along
The chorus of the song has gone
The stolen lives of those you've left behind

Temeraire

Horizon, sunset on the horizon
Light scattered falling from the sky
Reflections, ships on the water
Shorelines, cityscapes; fade, fade away

Orange, yellow, ochre, rust, blue
Flames flare from her chimney
As she tugs the majestic sailing ship
Underneath a sky with sun, with moon

Did he ponder on the galley
Wondering why not a soul in sight
Could the sea have been so many colours
Would that the imagination beamed so bright

From across the oceans, sailors gather
Line the decks as they reach the shore
Yesterday was flags and bunting
Today is calm, good men quietly go

Storm clouds behind the night
Bring brightness to the fore
Light, a likeness to your image
Your sun drenched early evening sky

Mandolin wind, you have the weight
Strings whispering, you are so so nearly being
Drum skins smoothed, brushstrokes wavered
The bass guitar plays, you gently weep, you cry

Promenader's right behind you
Waiting, watching your vision unfold

Your story you gave us on the canvas
Eight score years or more ago

Reds, greys, silvers, whites, golds
The flickering flag atop the mast
Ropes, rigging tidier than nature
Close up close I spy a crew

A sea of two-tone reflections
Mirror sun, mirror moon
Painting thousands of projections
For the nation to consume

Did you say you were going nowhere
No more the sea to be a roving
The last voyage has been taken
The last journey gone

We should have seen the sadness
The colour was without your joy
The smokestack racks our guilt
Cracks upon, our mistaken preconceptions

Haikuish

Drops of dew glisten
Stars trapped in the dawn day sun
A strangers galaxy

Reservoirs covered in snow
Icicle man astride
The pedestrians fluid divide

Bach of beach seasons
Surf over summers tales of reason
Blues sail on the perilymph

Dust To Dust

Sand dunes
You were on my mind
Seeing straight through
The soles of my shoes
Sand dunes
You were on my mind

Another quay
Another other time
Seeing beyond youth's truth
The midlife, in life, sayer-sooth
Another, another quay
Journey's, journey's lost in time

A glimpse behind the shoulder
Silk-scarf, swirling in the breeze
Laughter passing by there
Friends with all she meets
Perhaps she will look this way
Maybe she just might

Sand dunes
You were on my mind
Sand dunes
Looking back in time
Way down there, by the waltzer
Cheesecloth, crumbs of cheesecake

Taffeta, shiny glowing toffee apples
Joy unadorned, also candy-floss
Perhaps she will look this way
Maybe she just might

Sand dunes
Forgotten tunes

Remaindered runes
Stillness soon
Sand dunes
You were on my mind
Sand dunes
Journey's lost in time

Crescent Moon

I don't know when I lost you
Or when I lost myself

Beneath the crescent moon
Bathed by clear night stars

I don't know when I lost you
Or when you lost yourself

Rivulet

Wave crash
Whiplash, onward unknown soldier
Wave crash
Sea-splash, oceans growing older

Salt water drains across the bitumen tarmac
Lit by starlight, by streetlight going nowhere
Rain water drains into rivulets
Hiding moss grown stones, rolling over

Wave crash
Pebbledash, inward, homeward, boulder
Wave crash
Cars smash, societies apart, growing colder

Revealed

Knocked about, rough edges smoothed over
Rough diamond, a touch too smooth
Shaped by all that society could muster
Trusted too many pamphlets, too many books
Stripping bare is not an alternative
For the king already without his clothes

Masthead

Flags in the park
Bring light to dark
Reflection, stark realisation
Miles of orange cloth
Unveiled, curtailed
Sails for a city's soul's salvation
Creation, a core-declaration
Stores of ideas, enthusiasm's
Making something solid
Plastic, clay, vision
Monumental decision
Open to derision
Abounding in joy
Abounding with joy

Clear Water

Bhagavad Gita

Same as it is

Same as it ever was

Behind Proust

Approaching Evelyn Waugh

Pennies from Heaven

From five to eleven

Just too many coincidences

Sixth and seventh senses tell me

Remonstrate, castigate

Harden up the will

Forge some strata

Put some clear water

Between the you and the you

Vorticisize

Praxitella
Ample fella
Dynamist
Kissed by your own imagination
Kissed as a mistress
Kissed by your monumental sculptor

Beyond existence
Enlisted
All fingers fisted
Kissed by your picture
Your picture as a writer
Your writer as a picture

No wonder that you missed her
Kissed her like a sister
Realism
On society's cubist's blister
But the lines
They would not, could not go away

The lipstick
The saddened eyes
The emphasised thighs
With steely wrists
Gestures which suddenly kissed
Oh how much you must have missed her

Hair cropped
Shaped
From some pyramid scripture
No joy portrayed

Whoever was
The lear who kissed her

Tapping of the finger
Splinter
Through the window
My oh my
He almost missed her
Looking for her sister

Now you sit
In the dance club
Christ's entry into Jerusalem
Praxitella
Invaded on Jacob Kramer's
The Day of Atonement

Sputnik

The Navigation Arms
Let loose your senses
Released your defences
Of navigation

Nicotine, amber, creamy stout
Blackcurrant, cider, scallywags about
Mingling in with the inn crowd
Sing along, sing along Tom Dowd

Unsteadily stepping on the pebble shore
Pause, for a wee under the balustrade
Heads already beginning to thicken
Slow breathing, breathing clean seaside air

In the distance, listen; those screams of delight
Shivering, shaken, shaken out of the moonlight
Beach night, moonlight, starlight, summer flight
Listen to the screams, those screams of delight

Branscombe Beer, Plymouth Gin
Girls drink sin and tonic
We are only humans
This is no Sputnik, Brojnic

Back in this room, I've been here before
Eiderdown, radio, worn out floor
No one rings tonight, no one ever does
Words arise from below

Conversing, wandering, escaping
Philandering along the promenade

Planning permission is applied for
To turn it into flats

The locals complain out loud
But they haven't, have they
They have never stayed here
They've never crossed the threshold

Into this ancient, decaying ,dilapidated space
Some say they're business folk that run it
In it for what they can
In fact that's why I stay here

Not to be distracted
But to feel the man
To feel the man
Who also is neglected

It's closing time at the Navigation
It's closing time at the Bay Hotel
Close these places slowly
Close these spaceless souls so so slowly

Swinburne And Shandy

Swinburne
You could have been Mandy
Feverishly dandy
Tristram Shandy
Curvaceously randy
Down at the sandy
Turn
Of the tide

Your words, your expressions
Your suggests, your suggestions
Meter to measure
Disparate pleasure
Turn of the tide

Swinburne
Ever so handy
You are my eye candy
Extremely bandy
Thinner than Ghandi
Peter Pan or Andy
Turn
Of the tide

Your thoughts of your thinking
Dry draughts for the drinking
Climbing, climbing then sinking
Pleasures of leisurely linking
Turn of the tide

Swinburne
Port wine with lemon

Squeezing in the sermon
Foraging in German
Wearing Ben Sherman
Drinking Bourbon
Turn
Of the tide

Your moods, as your manner
Eclectic life spanner
Tan into tanner
Janitor's Janner
Turn of the tide

Swinburne
Rough as with ready
Nothing's ever steady
Everything is heady
Leadbelly is leady
Rock n rollers Teddy
Turn
Of the tide

Seeing Is Believing

Darkness
Real Darkness
Black lines on black skies
Inside the womb
Inside the tomb
Darkness

Shaft of light
White light
White lines on a white sky
Outside the womb
Beyond the tomb
Lightness

Too Many Times Of Parting

Void, devoid of direction
Not even thoughts
Of a misconception
Vacuous open universe

Standing in that bedroom there
Not knowing where to turn
Late autumn, early evening
Too many times of parting
Starting over again, restarting

Sitting on the second seat there
On the train from nowhere
Mid winter, morning, day
Too many times of parting
Starting over again, restarting

Laying in that churchyard there
In the unknown village
Some summer Sunday afternoon
Too many times of parting
Starting over again, restarting

Sleeping on that single bed there
In the student's dormitory room
Spent it all, then spent some more
Too many times of parting
Start over again, restarting

Hollow Score

All that went before
Has gone
Gone before

Creation crept along
Slipped the sand
From beneath the shoes

Chapel, church
All that went before
Has gone before

Familiarity swept along
A carpet ride
From an hollow floor

Mother, Father
All that went before
Has gone, gone before

Cosmos

There's a thousand million
Sparkling tinkling waltzing refractions
There's a never ending chorus
Of pebbles, of waves

The zephyr's blown in over the Dolomites
Travelling with some softness, some certainty
The migration has begun
Freshwater havens, seaside lakes are forsaken

Cotton wool clouds
Around the sky blue sky, surrounding silver tints
Above, a thousand million, maybe even a zillion
Sparkling tinkling star bright illuminations

To Be Is Not Alone Enough

White board
Wipe away
Move on
Gone

You travelled through
Some deep synapses
Erase, erasure
To lose, your loss as saviour

Quarantine
Quarantine or delete
Loosening links
Leveraging linkages

Opening wounds
Bound
Sealed
Slowly healed

Turn to
To find a sense
To find a purpose
To be is not alone enough

Buy some time
Rebuild the memories
Work out the why
Anticipate the when

Steam Gallery

Electric blue
Surfing through
Singles night reflection
Circumspect introspection
Electric blue
Shining through

Never seen your light before
Transmitting at the shore
Winters night
Transparent sight
Never seen you so bright
Before

Eclectic hue
Dancing shoe
Painter from the peak
Horizons you seek
Shine on through
Electric blue

Reading Maps Is Fun

Knot, intertwining, we'll meet you later on
Somewhere round the blowing house
Over Norsworthy Plantation way

Dwell, continue, we'll rest awhile
Beside the pixies house
Together on Yellowmead Down

Rustle, acquiring, we'll steal our herd our way
Through Woodtown then Furzetor Pass
Twixt here to Sampford Spinney

Dam, earth, buttress; we'll construct to confine
From the cattle grid to the homesteads
Under the shade of Combestone Tor

Quarry, excavate, we'll extricate information, to find
A way up Rugglestone Rock, to Seven Lords lands
Before we rendezvous at Widecombe in the Moor

Drink, libation, we will soon be there for prayer
Nearby the weir of Higher Coombe
Falling upon Scorriton, upon Scorriton Chapel

Mill, alcohol still, Benedictine of Buckfast
We'll make our way into a Cistercian Monastic order
Beside the Butterfly Farm near the Railway Museum

Steady

Rush
Without rapture
Straight
Into unravelling

Mall Today

Dear diary
Went to the mall today
Me and Molly Flanders
Suspicion surrounded, swept over our every move

All as gone before
That's gone before
All as gone
Gone that's gone before
All as gone before
Gone that's gone before

Masquerade, minuet
Pickpockets at the mall today
Johnny, Jenny, taking nickel's, taking dimes
The punters never notice, even stand in line

Dear diary
Drew my dole today
Along with Francis of Assisi
Desperation descends, deepens every mood

All has gone before
That's all gone before
Gone, all gone
All has gone
All has gone before
Gone that's gone before

Spices, dyes, crimson from Aspen
Old market stalls at the mall today
Saffron, with Shandy make atmospheric chimes

Wandering folk don't notice; while away the time

Dear diary
Bought some coal today
Me, Mrs Thatcher, and that scary Mr Scargill
Confrontation threatened every altercation

All that's gone before
That's all that's gone before
All gone before
Gone, all gone before
All has gone before
Gone that's gone before

Eye Candy

Red stilettos
Right up to her thighs
My it's nice
To climb so high

Why oh why
Its really nice to climb so high

Leather boots
Ermine for the firming
Foaming at the lips
Kiss her on the pips

By God it's nice
To climb so high

Denim jeans
Fit and mean
Squeeze on back
Back to seventeen

My oh my, by the by
It sure is nice to climb so high

Away For Winter

Closed hotel
Who is in your bedrooms
Who is in your entrance halls
Who last closed your last closed door

So you've gone to the Costa Brava
Gone from your silver-service
Gone from your waiting on
Who called your last, last orders

Would you mind if we stayed a while
Sleep quietly in your bedrooms
Hold hands along your hallways
Pick up the post from behind your door

We'll send your cards to Costa Brava
We'll always be at your service
We'll not keep you waiting on
On those last nights without last orders

Last Dance

Brandy, Babycham
Beck's or Budweiser
Close fit chiffon dress
Play hard to get

Another Marlboro
Share a Camel Light
Saxophone silhouette
Play hard to get

A bead of sweat
Shaking snake
Dancing in the dark
Play hard to get

Squeeze tight
Last dance rites
Smooch close
Oh so glad we met

Light Headed

Could be just coincidence
Incandescent, irreverent coincidence
Elemental, heaven sent
Coincident

But there's got to be more, more to it
More than innocent
Innocent collisions
Driving these decisions

Then again, someone said
Seven stories told
No more to unfold
Whether the pages are paper, papyrus or gold

But there's got to be more, more to it
More than lost civilisations
Civilisation's, civilised creations
Creating these collisions

Well soon, so they say, we'll all be ether
Moments passed
Memories lapsed
Neither you, nor me, nor our soft, soft breath

But there's got to be more, more to it
More than these poet's predilections
Their convictions and descriptions
Describing their alchemic prescriptions

So I move my arm sideways
Through the fine air

Demonstrative, debonair

Yes, ether it's me, or it is the Corsair

Doubt, No

Mackerel on rye

Tinned in tomato sauce
Packet from the corner all night store

Sat at someone else's dressing table
Another person belongs this space

Could afford the best in town
I mean the most delicate delicatessen

Doubt, no

Choice

Swinburne, Shute

Faded paperback by Pan
Not for sale in Canada

Reading someone else's book
Another person belongs a requiem for a wren

Could afford the leather bound
I mean the signed first edition of *A town like Alice*

Doubt, no

Choice

Walls, Windows
Magnolia with Tartan

Basket weave, knotted pine

Someone else created this place
Another person belongs the kitsch, the swish

Could afford the penthouse suite
I mean the most existentialist royal Casino Royale

Doubt, no

Choice

Walking or waiting

Making the first move
Indecisive in the end

Someone else made the pace
Another person belong's your familiar place

Could have carried on
I mean continuing more than incremental growth

Doubt, no

Choice

Playa de El Paradisio

For you to lay back, to imagine
Benjamin Zephaniah painting his poems in the sand
Derek Walcott welcoming himself to his own door
That Mr Marley rumbling up the band

For you to extend your imaginary senses a little
Sultry sunrise cotton daybreak
Sweet potato, mango, fresh caught fish
Breakfast in between

Now you're getting the taste, beginning to feel
The heat rippled skyline over wave breaks
Hand-gliding, water-sliding, rapidos rising
Beach bum, guitar strums, Indian summer

It's not yet ten, in the morning that is
Tonight the moon will set real slow
The jazz boys brass will blow
Dances will be fast, as fast as lasers glow

Before that there will be oysters
As you look out over the bay
In musk bound, orange and yellow chiffon and taffeta
The boys with studded belts, with Cuban heels

So you take a cup of coffee
Draw on one more cigarette
You close your eyes so tightly
This morning moment, you simply shall not forget

PS
Up there in the mountains

There is another poet painting over us

Everyone who is anyone was his visitor

They would not, could not, let him be; oh let him be

I Sit Inside The Christian Fellowship Coffee Shop

I sit inside the Christian fellowship coffee shop
Amongst a melodramatic search for reason
Day dreams of retreat
Into sublime silent solitude

Sparrow crumbs of memories
In flight across my mind

I actually sit
Astride the easy rider metro double decker bus
Visualising heathers of golden crimson
That one day we may walk among together

Old And Cold

I want to hold your hand
I so so want
To hold
Hold somebody's
Anybody's hand

I am growing old
Without love my hands are cold

I want to hold your hand
I so so want
To hold
Hold somebody's
Anybody's hand

Rill, Rivulet

Taw head
River Erme

Cascades of a ritual, sacrificial passage
Swirling ponds of cold water, cold as ice
River, rill, rivulet
Cascade of a ritual
Sacrificial
Passage

Streams of consciousness
Trout, stickleback
Splash about
Games, games
By the rivers, by the streams
Streams of consciousness

Proclaim

Now my friend
Ob la di, ob la da
My friend we will be together at the end

Sunny Sunday morning, the sower reaps
Spring dawns across his meadow
Around the world a mother sleeps

The sunlight catches the variegated ivy leaf
The reflected, crackled, puzzled pattern
At least two sides to a life, my liege

Now my friend
Now my friend
My friend we will be together at the end

Past patches of frost covered snowdrops
Climbing around the growers greens
Around the world a lover weeps

But they are tears of joy
Tears with smiles as big as rainbows
At least five lives in each life he breathes

Ob la di, ob la da
Could go on forever, could go on so far
So far as love would let me be, be my friend

Sunny Sunday morning, way above the bay
One raft for forgiveness, one raft for escape
One raft for sharing, one raft for you my friend

By the lych-gate the parson is out calling
Calling all before, *"the spring it is arriving"*
But I'll go bless my own sweet lord, ob la di

From leaf remember lichen, fore or aft who knows
Clinging, thriving, imbibing on nothing more
Than life itself

Some sunny Sunday morning
Sprinkle dewdrops
Dewdrops at the shore

Around the world, across a continent or more
Enigma's engulf the ebb, the flow
Enriched in deepest dream-space

Lovers in love with life
Understanding if not knowing
Not yet knowing all the score

Now my friend
This is no incantation
No medieval or Gregorian chant

My friend
This is love for you
My friend on to the end

Then how can we all proclaim this
How, my liege my leaf
How can we share this gentle awakening

How may we release unbounded joy
My friend we can go singing

Go on singing, *ob la di, ob la da*

Thanks to The Beatles White Album
Also to the Sacred Souls of Vermont

Torn, Twisted, Love's Blind She Whispered

Spanish, Spanish dancer
Just by chance, bring romance her way

Cuban heels, belt studded with steel
Just a dancer, bring a chance her way

She packed her case in isolation
Insincere, her lines of desertion
Her package of devastation

It could have been the castanets
It could have been the Sangria

Cuban heels, he'd made her feel
Her troubadour of real surreal steal

She wiped a tear
Folded her cotton handkerchief just so
She was torn, though she had to go

It could have been anytime
It just happened to be that summer

Belt of steel
Alive to feel

Whispered silver clouds above her
Blind to recover
For her Andalusian lover

Airport

Afternoon
Falling towards evening
Passengers boarding
Lover's dreaming
Afternoon

Sitting there
Gazing stare
Waiting for boarding
Feeling belief in
Sitting there

Fly away
Escape today
Horizons new
Seascape view
Fly away

Rambling rose
No one knows
Your crimson clothes
Disguised from foes
My rambling rose

Stories told
Dreams unfold
Evenings cold
Sunsets of gold
Stories did unfold

I am Out Of Here

Your needs made clear
It's time to steer
A brand new course
Some fresh resource

I am on my way out of here
Where I go I have no fear
No desires lurking
Just keep on working

Keep on skirting around
What it was that bound me
Surround myself, be impressed
Forget, forgotten already the rest

You can check, you can test
I've finished with feeling second best
It's time to be clear
This path I steer

This lurking fear
This skirtings dear
Sounds around
Outward bound

I am impressed to clear
No more those words I fear
I am out of here
Yes, I am out of here

Abreast The Iron Radiator

I lay there sideways
Frying inside, lying on the floor
You were there
Lying somewhere, beyond the wall

Candles in the window
Silk, silk sheets, sunken satin bed
We lay apart, together yet miles away
You lie next door

Maybe that is all
All you ever wanted
To sleep alone, sleep for sure
Beyond those crazy midnight calls

Then the curse moved in with the treasure
Was it alcohol
Or was it rock and roll
Or was it just, just for sexual pleasure

In that museum place
A shelter, a rest
Away from London's pouring roaring rain
Alongside the dinosaur

Abreast the iron radiator
You fondled my balls
My fondled balls
Were put to your test

Before long we were lovers
Restaurant tables

Vomiting at the seashore
Caught up completely

We were little mother-fuckers
Now it's over, it's gone, it's over
Our stations are cold
Our dreamscapes we've strolled

We've created bronze from gold
Yet still the physical goes on
Last rites
Even after it's over

Proposing

Now I'm used up
Can I use you
Can I write all sorts of stuff

White mini-skirt
Tight around your thighs
Heels only just holding on

Flying to every party
Catching-up
On all that you thought you'd missed

Old men can't help
But be enchanted
When you blow smoke

Right through their eyes
Those younger men
Once besotted they can't ever let it lie

The older guys
They help with your pretending
That life's about something more

They blow to you
They go propose to you
Supposing that nothing's ever new

The Vase Will Not Be Broken

Old smoke stacks are burning
Their last coals of the day
The fires will be allowed to die out overnight
In the morning the kiln doors will be broken open

The class will express wonderment
Congratulate each other
On their various works of art
The art teacher will ache

For the student teacher's vase
She's here on placement
Teaching history
History shows he will have his way

The class of 67 will tease her
She will break down in tears
The students will join forever friends
Form an internet community

The lustful liaison will bear fruit
Miss Kelly will push Mr Ward
In his wheelchair
Along Brighton promenade

He will have a hand made rug on his lap
A sensitive placement
Their vase, not unlike history
Their vase will not be broken

Together alone

You are here
But I am alone
We are together here
Together alone

The spaces between the faces
Are further apart than they've ever been
We are being here being, being together alone

The words climb over the clifftops of our lips
And fall to the canyon floor below
We are here talking, separate sentences, words alone

You are here
But I am alone
We are together here
We are together forever, forever alone

Flesh and Rye

Around the maypole
Purple, blue, orange, yellow, multifarious garlands
Dance the dance of May, skipping in, skipping out
The maypole dance, skipping, sipping innocence

Or did you even then
Have your eye on V's tie dye

Around the rounder's base
Serge blue knickers, plimsolls and tee shirts
Pitch, swing, run, catch, throw, run, gasp, grasp
Run the rounder, round the son's of innocence

Or did you even then
Have your eye on Y's breast and thigh

Around the fields of canvas
Purple, blue, orange, yellow, beads and bandanas
Strum, chord, drum, strum, chord again
Strum the summer sun, summer sun of innocence

Even then it did you
Filled your eye, that festival of flesh and rye

Blind the philistines

Better lines than words
Better blind than absurd

Cuckold to this life passing by
Walking the bridle path
While the slow boats whistle by

Beside the fields of rye
Beside the towpath
Dreamboats and dream's hopes lie

Agent provocateur stimulates discussion
In the smoke filled rooms
Of dominoes, draught bitter, embittered delusion

Brighter lights and busy times
Brighter whites to blind the philistines

Fingers folded the clay that moulded

The clay
Moulded
Sculptured
Warmed
Caressed
Kissed and blessed

The fingers folded
Detail's scolded
In frustration
Hands
They are the artists enigma
To build them in a way to reflect a life

To show compassion
To show desire
Hands in motion
Yet still
Hands that work
And hands that kill

They are though for today art
Art for the gallery visitor
The register of culture in miniature
Yes today it's Modigliani and Epstein
The Pillars of Tenderness

Sussed not sassy

Recently presented resentment
Resent intended descent
Pretence suspended, no doubt depended

Wait, wait while I say
Wait, while I say, say
I'm at a loss, at a loss
I don't know what to say

Recently, in the not too too distant past
Presents were passed, cards were marked
Resentment if at large, was held at bay

Wait, wait awhile, wait, stay
Stay, wait, wait while I say
I'm at a loss
I don't know what to say

Re-sent the message not received
Intended for you found another
Descent delayed, laid upon the ledge's edge

Wait, stay, say, say awhile
Say, wait awhile, stay
I'm at a loss
I don't know what to say

Passing by

The stars are popping, skip hopping
Into the blood blue, blue night sky
A further station of the cross, it is show stopping
Mopping up the blessed, blest Pope John Paul

The shooting stars fly east to west
Fading aureole carried by the borealis
Boy I'm blest
I am no longer second best

Freed from among the rest
The night time test is going west
Boy I'm blest
I've flown the nest

Popping eyes
Stopping lies
Dropping why's
And hints of evermore

The blue night sky
She'll show me where to lie
Hang my hat beyond the falling star
I've travelled far

To lift this lowered bar
Back up aside the Byzantine tzar
Up into the ether
With John Paul meeting Peter

Exponential form

Colour; gold or silver or invisible white, I guess the truth is the colour was not seen.

But for arguments sake, and by the way there is no one here with which to argue, so there we have it, the colour was invisible bright white.

The weight was between weightlessness and an immoveable load, the burden though was fleet of foot and moving, moving to all parts of the physical being, seen through some 'in body' out of body experience.

So to give some basis for further thought, if that's ok, we'll give it the weight of the pulsating sheep's heart, pulsating in free gravitational space.

Mass, I guess, and force or distance travelled, combine to give some measure of energy or interpersonal, magnetic, dynamic pull.

Well it was here, there, took no time at all in flight, yet it consumed all around, and filled every void, it was the size of a cloud bursting, a cloud filling the soul.

In this case to add to the algorithm, or the proposition; call it if you will, we will give it the dimension of an almost round-cornered trapezoid in elemental, five dimensional space.

In these modern times communication engulfs nation over nation, yet this creation held the communication platform by its own choice, for its own time, without duplex or duplicity, no modem held it bound.

For it is power of thought transmission we will, I'm sure you will agree, then give it a level of an infinite skill.

There we have it then, we've got some components to consider, all that's left is the combination.

But unfortunately, as fast as we can create and combine, we must be aware that there is a strong destructive force not far away.

The next bit though is for you boys and girls to take on and complete.

All I'll do for now is give, give, me being a generous sort, I will give you one of many possible endings:

Pulsating at the pace of the dying heart, pulsating and fading like a decaying amplitude modulation, slowly arising, slowly declining, slowly disappearing, slowly reappearing, peering in decaying exponential form.
In that one moment; here, and gone.

Sixteen's the word

It has been sixteen years I'd say
Sixteen years I've been losing my way
It's sixteen years
Sixteen years to the very day

And sixteen years before that score
Sixteen years plus some more
Another sixteen years
Sixteen years leading again, out of the door

Then sixteen years, before some more decayed
Sixteen years or more I'd stayed, stayed and played
With my mother and her lover of sixteen years
Sixteen years of unconditional love she gave

Escaping Away

It has been a busy day
I have escaped a long long way
Early on I was talking to Mr. Masefield
Resplendent in his business black suit

The cut was neat, lined with finest silk
The hair was brave, not a Locke did misbehave
He was with Elisabeth, is it Mrs. Stanhope Forbes
By the edge of the woods, turkey crop and scythe

They were wondering at the Moonlit View
Of Mr. Francis Darby's Eastern city
As they dared to forsake, partake
In Mr. Geoffrey Hill's grinning cake

In the background, surround sound all around
Beside you, sang Mr Van Morrison, oh *Astral Weeks*
It has been a very busy day
I have escaped ever such a long long way

Journeyed almost as far as Camilla
Who married again, this day, today
I did not go to the service
I spilt my tears among the radio congregation

Tears of joy and there but for the grace of god go I
Or is it the North Wind
Blowing alongside the dust ball, to the canal basin
That which I am to engage with, in regeneration

A long term plan, you say
I retort, as if Capability Brown ever saw

His landscapes as anything more than nature
In full sway, in full public awe

Here in Weston Park, under the mid-day
Noon time dark
Clouds, clouds with Eastern rain
And Southern comfort

It has, as I say, been a long long day
I've escaped, escaped in a very busy way
Before meeting Mr Masefield
I'd scribed a few words of my own

Memories of yesterday's funeral
Polish youth, in Polish dress, the Pope was thus blest
Memories of yesterday's other funeral
The receivers set the works to rest

Oh and lest I forget
I'd imagined and spoken, words under my breath
I'd spoken, under my breath
Another day, escaping death

It has been such a long day
Escaping in many a different way
Unlike the child dying in St. James Hospital
By the Poet's hand in the library compilation

'Out of Fashion' I recall the cover rolled
Although I did not study the small print
I did though take the flyer
To hire a china dragon, a dragon blowing fire

And I bought some books, go on, take a look

Yes it is John Stammer's 'Stolen Love Behaviours'
And Jackie Kay's *Life Mask*, although I thought
The cover was an Eduardo Palozzi creation, it was in
fact clay

And finally *Scenes from Comus* by Geoffrey Hill
Ticked by the Archbishop of Canterbury no less
It has been, as once again I say
It has been a long day

It is not yet noon, although it will be evening soon
Beneath the midnight of the moonlit moon
Except that today, yes today of all days
Today I am escaping away

Reaping Rake

Your lips were shielded
My attempted kiss was fielded
I was at mid-on, you were in the deep
Have you lost the ache
Or did I make a mistake
Was another known, sown to reap

Your lips were dry
My finger tips did try
I was in a spot; you were playing a sideways shot
Have you lost the ache
Or did you make, on purpose take
A solemn aplomb chastity vow

Your body wandered
My advances squandered
I was seeping, you were wicket-keeping
Have you lost the ache
Or were you playing the long game
No time for a quick one, as slow coming she came

Your last defence was tested
Tip of tongue, engaging, redemption rested
Your lips moist to wet, tongue tip nest and set
Was it lust or just a mistake
Afterwards you, did you ache
One more fallen swollen reaping rake

Watercombe; Thirteen years and more ago

And today in my mind I am revisiting
Just for you, oh, and also for me

I came to this place
Almost twenty three months ago
Then, as now, the sky was blue
The river tumbled and splashed

Like a poet planted
Some time before the snow
Blue, blue, big blue Friday afternoon
Beside the lonely, the only one, the River Erme

In between the then and now
Turbulence has been maintained
Turbulent mind, turbulent body
Turbulent health, turbulent wealth

From landing to leaving
Things were fluid and rolling
My head was full of love, my body was tired or alive
I was ill, I was well, I was poor, I was paid

The sheep graze these windswept moors
Lambs born amongst the driving rain
Alongside the gorse and the reeds
A crop cut grass pleads to grow

Those crazy beasts keep on mowing
There love-stock are dropped and fawned
Where it's rough it's ready
Why should we ever misconceive

And the bleat breaks
That waterfall of springtime silence
Alone amongst a thousand acres
Chasing after mother, after mother nature

No more whingeing or whining
Springtime springs once again
In a world beyond the shoulder
Whatever we can believe, she can give more

Talking

It used to be so easy to make the call
So easy to start the talking

Space here for several years of failing love

But now talking of what
Small talk to just keep talking

I forget

Our love has now departed
It lies there, the living dead
I forget how it started
Was it said, or left unsaid

It's time for moving on
It lies there, left to fester
I forget how to start
Was it a now, or later on

It's not a new beginning
It lies there, begun before
I forget the lines and timing
Was it, have you been no more

It's weird, just not to know
It lies there, untouched
I forget spontaneous smiles
Was it forged, for all who flushed

It's floating on grey clouds
It lies there, like the drizzle rain
I forget springtime sunshine
Was it grey, in the evermore of pain

It's taking your turn always
It lies there, waiting on
I forgot, I forget
I am, moving on

Seeing through to pray

Mist
Morning around dawn
Waters edge ripple
Moorhens dip, swans neck's flip
Springs nature ramble trip
Before the morning tipple

Mist, silver grey, early day
Fields of hay, curds and whey, mist

Morning
Dawning around daylight
Shafts of light, lover's flight
Losing sight, ever might
A little tight
Drizzle another tipple

Mist, smoky haze, early days
Funny ways, window bays, mist

Waters edge ripple
Scattered pebbles and tickled trout
Vibrating pulsating waves, waves about
Echoes shout; ale and stout, ale and stout
Cast a clout
Undress and pour another tipple

Mist, white noise, kick and poise
Slick Latin boys, big girl's toys, mist

Moorhens dip, swan neck's flip
Underneath, above, below as above

Preening dove, fallen love
Push and shove
Form a queue
Queuing for another tipple

Mist, sea frets and cloud covered sunsets
Place your bets, take the test, mist

Springs nature ramble trip
Refreshing souls feeding salvation
Wonderment creation, the crosses station
Exceeding expectation, tingling sensation
Tipping at Temptation Lake
Aching for another tipple

Mist, fuddled mind, blinded from behind
Forgotten kind, clocks to wind, mist

Before the morning tipple
Last night's wasted way
Yesterday's forgotten day
Job gone, no more pay
House lost, no where to stay
Except for another tipple, oh pray

Mist

Donald Shimoda

Just along the A5
Past Weston Park
An early morning drive
Ripe to be surprised

Inner self or outer self
Collective unconscious
Or something deeper
Daffodils in bloom deep within
The sunken soul

Like a ghost
Or a drowned man floating to the surface
The movement was a continuum
Without jar or jolt, the rising
Om, Om, Om for a lost love

Later, in peace, quiet, calm, tranquillity
Om cannot resurrect
From the pit of the body to the tip of the mind
There is no traffic to carry the urn of any kind

The ashes have flown on the wind
Unable to rescind the cindered lingered candle
A flickering, flickering, sickening, failing glow
Extinguished, vanquished, decayed
A dying atmospheric orb

But it did happen
And for that I thank more than I can ever know
I write these words of thanks
To tell you, of what I do not know

Is that how the flower feels in pollination
Some union with an Albion of kind
Was it received or reciprocated or was it bounded
Then bandaged; was it unrequited love

Like the kite blown along the breeze
Or Donald Shimoda in timeless flight
It is a Messiah's handbook which helps me discover
To recover the greetings of souls; souls meeting
Greeting together as deep below; below as above

Wasted Place, Sometime

Somewhere on the M5
Around Taunton way I'd say
The morning after nothing had happened

The blue, clear blue sky
Matched the mood of release
Relief from those scattered sheets

That dripping tap
Shrinking threads and wasting washers

Now I remember
Before Bristol for sure, the afternoon before
The night when nothing happened

The grey sea mist from the estuary
Matched the mood of doubt, unknown quarry
Set up for the fall, recall the previous dishes.

That silken strap
Silken threads and tummy squashes

Now I remember
Down among the Chilterns
The evening, the actual evening, the non event

If it meant anything, It meant nothing to me
The wind drifted, the rainbow lifted
Lifted on moor and gorse

No recourse, no negotiation, a stated situation
Inclined by inclination I'm listening to Bukowski

You're watching television, you're watching TV

Now I remember
Some place obscure
Wasted time for sure

Sex, whore, wife, life
How would it feel to think your wife a whore
Lore would life suffice such a trice

Would the expectation stride in tight
At the fleeting sight
Of the translucent gossamer light

Wobbly

Wobbly
Sleeping together
Keep your distance
Close your eyes to realise
The futile situation
A brutal station
Mutual pain
Acrid Rain
Singles dance
Lost romance
Do not touch
Do not chance
Being kind
Keep a cool mind
Calm emotions
Steady nerves
Don't stir it up
Do not stir it up
So tired
Little time left to sleep
Anxieties awakened
Temperance shaken
Sleeping together
Oddly
Wobbly

Smothered lovers

Naked
Never
Except forever
When we were lovers

Together we discovered
We smothered our bodies with love and lust

Naked
Cleverly
We revealed
Our concealed others

Together we stroked and smoked
Hoped without talk to recover our lust and love

Naked
Together
Under natures covers
We were, weren't we, we were smothered lovers

Posing Nude

She more than made an effort, her figure creator. Every morning not yawning, but slipping on the tummy vibrator. Melba toast was the most that passed those sweet red lips. Palates, yoga, stretching, swaying, swaying those swinging hips.

The artists and the painters they did not restrain her. Posing nude for her life class and for her figure friend dude. Running on the moors, treading timeless, line-less steps. Pumping iron, and swimming on, down the full length lane.

Fully spread under summer sun, tanning, figure slamming. Cramming in the cranberry juice and the fat free yoghurt. All of this to manage the refrain between size twelve and size fourteen

Skin supplements, perpetual E45. Conscientiously keeping her beauty, keeping beauty alive. The hairdressers kept moving, they were kept on their toes. A trim, a bob, no perm, for my brunette, well trimmed rose.

At the dogs again

The steam room and the sauna
They are my racetrack, my sweet fleeting fauna
The swimming pool and the meditation star
They are my cigarette, my whisky, my pimp, my bar

Now this simple phraseology, this word psychology
This is my style, not yours, for that I make no apology
The tidy quiet room; laid back jazz and soulful blues
This is my non-hovel, I have no desire to grovel

Yet I read your works and marvel at your creation
Your escapades; words, to which I bear no relation
But just to put your mind at rest, in you I did invest
In the Jacuzzi; the plumes sure do dress the nest

The volva, the vulva caressed by volcanic water vests
Tattoos on thighs open your eyes, stir feelings blest
And their are girls there with their mothers
And ladies going on girls, there with their lovers

The lecher stretching don't take much fetching
When there's so much skin, skin waving, shaving skin
For inspiration and amusement, when in lent
The spa's the place to rent

For feelings, or ejaculations mistakenly spent

Thought transference

You thought your way into my thoughts
And you fought your way right out again
It was your thinking not your drinking
That propped me, stopped me from sinking

Your critical, cryptic crossword completion
Revealed, your subtle sense of reason
And your letters, your letters though sparse and thin
Your written words sold me, fever rising, muse within

Your turn of phrase with unnerving staring gaze
Razor sharp, cutting; may I mention tension raised
The gifts you gathered, the detail mattered
Thoughtful choices, so soft and carefully scattered

Even now on leaving
Misbelieving there's no articulated deceiving
Your thoughts I'm holding high
In my sinking, slinking, thinking

Come to terms

I'd forgot to grieve
Got up to leave
A mumbling stumbling goodbye

I'd not taken the time to cry
Too busy asking why
Caught up in my own insensitivity

Reading some other folks words
Looking at nature, studying birds
Wallowing in the following wind

Now it's time to come to terms
Wash those wicked feelings, terminate the germs
Wish you all the best, with sincerity

I'm in the country and visiting the city
Writing and reading, words full of self pity
Drinking coffee and smoking cigarettes

The world has become my oyster
That's a tricky one, choices can loiter and be foisted
So I'll catch their word, hoping that's not too absurd

Low flow the high blow

Low blow the high flow
Trip the tease that strips to please
Low flow the high blow

Waters edge the bather's pledge
Strip to please the tease that trips
Waters pledge, the bather's edge

Low flow the high blow

Void

Words without ideas
Words without love
Ideas without love, without words

Mute
Brute
Scoot
Shoot

Thoughts without thinking
Thoughts without drinking
Thinking without drinking, without thought

Dupe
Sloop
Troop
Stoop

Sight without seeing
Sight without being
Seeing without being, without sight

Blind
Mind
Find
Behind

Wireless spokes

Lightness after loss
Hope after dark
Life after all

Unchained, free, freed
From inert confusion
Delusion dispersed

Lightness before daybreak
Sleep with dreams
Sleep in peace

Unchained, released restraint
From created capture
Rapture reneged

Lightness during dawn and dusk
Walking without shadows
Walking with angels

Unchained, clasps recycled
From twisted thoughts
And wireless spokes

Lightness under the sun
Lightness under the moon
Lightness, not a moment too soon

Oh sweet gentle morning

Oh sweet gentle morning
Oh sweet water flowing
Cross pastures and meadows
Sweet breezes blowing

Sun bright, clear sunlight is shining
Blue, blue sky, fresh breath is aligning
Oh sweet gentle morning
Oh sweet water flowing

Along by the seashore
Eating mackerel on rye
Over blue misty mountains
Under cool wispy fountains

Oh sweet gentle morning
Oh sweet water flowing
From Arizona to Egypt
The rock face and the delta

The air we are breathing
The clothes we are weaving
Oh sweet gentle morning
Oh sweet water flowing

In Piccadilly Circus
Over Wordsworth's London bridge
The tourists are flocking
The Cafes and pavements are rocking

Oh sweet gentle morning
Oh sweet water flowing

The sculptures are fondled not fumbled
The galleries are wandered and wondered

Expressions of beauty
Of love and desire
Oh sweet gentle morning
Oh sweet water flowing

And now we'll take tea
Our oat cakes by the fire
We'll open the paper
Enjoy the magazine *The Wire*

Oh sweet gentle morning
Oh sweet water flowing

Sacred events and sacraments

How to describe the path
Along the load less travelled
Caress the odd Hesse less journey
As it is, as it ever was

Sacred coals burnt, scorched
No more imaginary goals
From now on it's sacred events and sacraments
It is, it is as it is, it is as it never was

Eye, seeing eye; eye, seeing
By being, by being by the day
There to say to be, and to be being
To cry, cry to the heavens and the skies

Me, my, oh me, oh my
My oh my
Me, why
Oh me, oh why

A funny sort of Therapy

A funny sort of therapy
Remember; rubbing pebbles from the beach
This time
It is all in the mind
A different kind of therapy
A full blame culture
Tearing like a vulture
Unloading every which way
Unloading each and every day
Unloading with no reprise, in full sway
Unloading without relent
Unloading cares away

A funny sort of therapy
Remember; we weren't allowed to be alone
This time
Not trying to be kind
A different mind for therapy
Another game culture
Tear apart the vulture
Scolding, no pain withholding
Scolding, each day unfolding
Scolding, with no restraint for full to slay
Scolding without relent
Scolding cares away

Another sort of touching

I was trying to remember
What it was like to fall in love
I was lying here looking
Ogling at that turquoise top
Staring at that flash of flesh, Gilgamesh
Was I confusing
Was I abusing
Abusing lust, lust with love

And then I remembered
Remembered that Sunday morning
Flight lands and arrives, landing with nowhere to go
I was just in place, some place, anyplace
Wandering, in love, in love with a big grin

OK so we'd made love some time earlier
And that was some, that was some intoxication

Still, even with intoxication
This was some other sort of touching
Another sort of touching
Touching that caught
Caught, captured in rapture
On a rapturous Sunday morning

The purple haze had descended
My mended mind remembered
Every touch, every stroke
Every word we spoke
Spoke throughout the night
Spoke way on into the morning
Way on into the morning

And when we rose for the sunrise
To skip along the sands
In nothing more than our bare feet
Nothing more than our love
Our kissing
Kissing, kissing, sweet kissing sunrise

Sunrise that burnt off the hazy night descended
My mended mind remembered
Sitting by the ebb tide
Feeling for toes, toes toasting in the sunlight
Feeling another sort of touching
Another sort of touching

Was I touching
Was I touching love

Or is my memory fed
Bled
Bled dry
Dry with lust
Not Love

Carpets of thorns and lilies

Other Men's words
The kerbstones that I've misplaced
Searching their words, for rhyme or reason
Staining seasons passed, it's now clearer space

Gravestones and epitaphs
Inscriptions defy descriptions, of the words I'm after
Gathering spontaneity, picking grave to grave
A kaleidoscopic conversation, a generation saved

The lilacs and the bluebells, cards from Mrs May
Carpets of bluebells, thorns and lilies; far away days
Of all the deaths you've told and listened
All the bouquets you've pondered and passed

You've read other men's words
Passed their pasts, into some unknown future place
Searched their faces for rhyme or reason
Staining seasons passed, a new 'to begin' space

Footnote

The first poem in trying to break away from the poetry of the past, that morning I'd written a few words of closure (however temporary) on a past relationship, I'd read a little of Adrian Henry, and halfway through typing up the poem Mr Van Morrison came along, singing of Madame George. The following 24 poems are from a vacation in Kos immediately after this idea to change.

A quiet conversation

A quiet conversation
A silent contemplation
Wind chimes, slow days
Passages in time
Wind, blowing sweet softly
Sage, rosemary and thyme

A quiet conversation
Morning light, morning
A silent contemplation
Morning light, morning
Holding hands
On Giants Causeway
Footprints wander this way
In the sand

A quiet conversation
A silent contemplation
A quiet conversation
Morning light morning
Trickling stream
Over bouldered rock
Poppy, fetlock
Gaze over the meadow

A silent contemplation
Morning light morning

Stuttering Staccato

She wrote me a letter
Talked of garlands and May
Walk with me through the meadow
Tread with me softly, she did say

I replied in stuttering staccato
Struck a strangers chord, with echo and delay
Your kindness, gentle, finds and swamps me
I'm sinking fast, I did say

She wrote such words that turned me
Talked of where, and when we'd play
Talked with me so full of passion
She'd twist the vine with me, she did say

I replied by post, almost rolled over
Searching deep for every word
Your passion fever, finds and haunts me
My writing is past, you'll find I did say

Glowing at the attention

A little sad reflection
Fifteen years ago this day
In the land of Mr Pye
Building castles in the sand

The horse drawn carriage beckoned
Children's bonnets and the sun cream for protection
Protection needed you had reckoned
On this island free, free to begin, to begin to dream

We wandered up towards the headland station
We gazed the azure blue over to France
This was our first vacation
A consolidation of subterfuge romance

Laying in the meadow dozing
Clumps of Jasmine beneath the peregrine by chance
Laying on the meadow headland dozing
Taking photos of sparrows doing their 'flutter dance'

We'd travelled on the hydro foil of Condor
Sat on the deck in Channel Island sunshine
The light of lightness being longer
Holding hands in some pave crazed expectation line

We had the corner table
The restaurant was first class
The girls glowed at the attention
And you glowed at their sass

We played some games a little later
Scrabble, and cards; was it Twist or was it Fish

Oh so happy, even before our consummation
We were feeling, feeling lovingly rich

And when we had returned
The photographs cannot lie
I was caught adrift and snoozing
You as ever, were camera, camera shy

Now it's another May Day holiday
An island by the name of Kos
No longer at one together; here tonight without you
Remembering what, oh what on earth it is we've lost

Being tougher might have been kinder

Being tougher might have been kinder
Maybe I could have been kinder to myself

I could have seen the end before it happened
But suspended, I gave myself just too much rope

Was it the rough ride that life had bled for you
Did my chase relent to eventually embrace you

Being tougher might have been kinder
We could have been kinder to ourselves

We could have seen the end before it happened
Suspended, each kept on giving just too much rope

Archangel Michael

On board
On board the Archangel Michael
Kos, a present from the English
For helping win the freedom war
Took from 45 to 58 to get the papers sorted
On board
On board the Archangel Michael

An anchor slip on the wooden ship
Island sun, nun forsaking nun
The purple sage has read you
The sprigs and the twigs are to tread through

On board
On board the Archangel Michael
A floating boat of hope
Worry beads, religions icons, photos of the pope
And Greek Orthodoxy for the crew
On board
On board the Archangel Michael

A landing stage for boats to lay
A slip of sand, a welcome hand
The island blade has read you
The boats and warmer coats
We're all just floating through

Nigh on caught the writers eye

The purple pink ink was sprinkling
Words deeper than the page could print
The deep red sun in the sky was sinking
Skies hues bluer than the blackest ink

The vermouth gin was drinking
Crazed, laced, aniseed, menthe and mint
The blue black sky had summers stars a twinkling
Skies light, whitest snowball cocktail drink

The drink distilled the multicoloured inks
The pink blue sky nigh on caught the writers eye
The instinct was to close, the amber nectar rose
A painter shaped his pose, a poet had another drink

Sweet memories being mended

My befriended mind descended
Lent itself a favour, or was it two

The bitterness is ended
It could not, could not be defended

My censored mind now is scented
Meant for long to labour
Except that now it is all spent through

The bitterness is indeed near on ended
Now it's the sweet memories
My sweet memories being mended

But truly there's no fever crazy

And still I go on floating
I can't explain the feeling so
But you can tell from my writing
It's not too too easy letting go

But truly there's no fever crazy
Nothing's driving me, not live nor lazy
No absence making feelings fonder
No loss or absent mind to wander

It's a most unusual face, to face
In the morning when I've slept well
I just get on with what I have got to do
No remorse or rekindling, hurts not breaking through

But I know it's not me that's holding
Lack of scolding feeling not of my conscious making
Yet something else, something unknown is going on
For how long, how long, how long, how…

Singers And Songs

Singer
Sing your sweet songs
Your hallelujahs
Your California dreaming
Singer
Sing your sweet songs

Oh Spanish guitar
Strum your tune away
Your footsteps in the sand
Your castles and diamonds
Oh Spanish guitar
Strum your tune away

Mocking bird
Fly your wings away
Here to stay
Here till Saturday
Mocking bird
Fly your wings away

Surest love

It is her surest love
That is what she's surest of
He's home to stay
Never gonna go away
Her sad refrain
He'll soon be back again

And surest love
What are those words you say
You were singing yesterday
Never gonna go away
Then that railway train
Will he ever be back again

Hear that mellow blow
From the horn and the piccolo
Surely, she's lost her surest love
Downtown now he's a gigolo
With her he's left his lust-filled stain
As if forever, oh will he be back again

She mourns the loss
On this isle of Kos
She'll paint again
Lover's love she will abstain, abstain
She will still feel the pain
Ever will he, ever be back again

The boats have sailed
He's left no mail
His muse and his minder
He's off across the seas to find her

Remind her of the heroes he has slain
Never, not ever, never to be back there again

Strummer

Oh Grecian summer
Began with yon Joe Strummer
His Spanish ways, oh Spanish days
Clash boys clashed from London to Andalusia

Now he's passed away
His Mescalano's have had their day
He's moved right on, he's left his all
The back catalogue of a music lover

Silver threads upon the Rockies

Crumbled stone
Jumbled civilisation

Lemon grass among the poppies
Sandstone slate and marble

Worry beads, windblown seeds
Fish, bird, goat, hashish

Crumbled tome
Jumbled imagination

Silver threads upon the Rockies
Image, vision, thoughtless sparkle

Nervous weeds, unknown creeds
Idea, gift, wrath, blessing, pathways

Forlorn four leaf clover

Daisy chain, one more refrain
Forlorn four leaf clover

Buttercup, something's coming up
Sojourn, among the pampas

Herb garden, Cardigan bay
Mourn, a summer's lover's passing

Cabbage patch, locks off the latch
Storm brewing, crow clouds in the sky

Potato fields, his torch she wields
Warm autumn's harvest festival

Bridge across the sky

Thousands of miles away
Across so so many seas
Where are your thoughts at this moment

Can you stop, just now
Think of this place
Across so so many seas

Take a moment
A small mobile meditation
Close your eyes
Bridge across the sky

Thousands of miles away
Your muse, your love, your tree
Across so so many seas

Did you feel the fleeting thought
Grasp that visualisation flash
Across so so many seas

Less than separate minds
In splitting seconds bind
Touching skins together fly, bridge across the sky

Thousands of miles away
Your friend, your love, your free
Across so so many seas

Caught that synapse strobing
Mind depths you were probing
Together, across so so many seas

Now there's intermingling

Souls engaged, lattice leaves, layers lingering

Open your eyes; you've bridged across the skies

Leaving gaps to wander through

Your mind was searching
For your favourite song
But you needed peace and quiet
Or some divine intervention

Those days you tripped
Your memory slipped
Turned down a gear or two
Leaving gaps to wander through

Your mind was searching
It's become a fashion thing to lose
You do it with a passion
Like a fever not to choose

Those days you dipped
Those drinks you sipped
Slowed down the inner you
Leaving gaps to wander through

For Mark

Not lonely, moments

These only, not lonely
My own
Only
Not lonely, moments

Only my own
Once lonely
Now only
My own, not lonely, moments

Moments
My own
Only my
My moments

Only, only
My only
My own
Moments only

Our dreams to longer ponder

For those of us, who are boys no longer
Those boys and girls, who are only left to dream
Boy, she sure brings those dreams much more closer
Close and mean she brings along the longer dream

For days and daze in summer sun she wanders
Days to see, to dream our old forgotten dreams
A skin of silk, a bosom without blemish
Thongs embrace, place for dreams to longer ponder

Oh yellow frock, your smock don't shock or mock me
My feelings peel, I steal away to in my dreams reveal
A cappuccino, a writer's hand upon my shoulder
Boy, I'm growing older, pray fold away my dreams

It's coring though not screaming

I core away my evening
I core away, to try to find a feeling
Revealing evening's feelings
Coring through the old grey ceiling

Sealing the old but not forgotten feelings
Although without today, they have no meaning
Just before the time for dreaming
I am coring, stealing, and reeling

It's coring though not screaming
It's welcoming not scheming
It's opening and it's leaving
Leaving you, to encompass you, in my dreaming

It's a tightrope life I'm living

It's a funny path to tread
Trod with boots of lead
We never really said
Goodbye

Now we are just not talking
Lifting the telephone but choking
Dark nights alone chain smoking
Goodbye

Fearful for and of the future
Careless with the lucre
Time turns sour not sucre
Goodbye

My words through my mind are sieving
This tightrope line, it's a tightrope life I'm living
Hope is here, oddly so so often it is forgiving
Goodbye

It always turns into a poem

It always turns into a poem, it must mean, mustn't it,
that there is something else within, anyway, for now,
I'm trying to write about something strange,
something far from known before, or not even half
understood, some strange feeling.

It's not anger, and it's not loss; there is a deal of not
living up to reality, there is a deal of keeping your
image alive, but it is not yet, at least I hope, not yet an
infatuation.

And that's the thing that scares me, in this what is
almost calm serenity; do I risk rolling over to an
hungry infatuation, do I risk that, by keeping your
image alive.

By using you for my poetry, for writing down and
remembering, I'm seeing you each evening, and
taking you to my dreams, do I risk an hungry
infatuation, that will eat me, eat me half alive.

Or is this path truly more cathartic, is it a passage
towards a closure, will this calm feeling of now grow
into something stronger, bringing me, giving me,
without you forever, leaving me, giving me new
hope.

More frightened still to ask

I am writing this in Kos
With you it would have been…
For me now it is time with Andrew
And a little time with me

I don't know what you're feeling
I'm scared now to ask
I'm frightened to see a closure
More frightened still to ask

Far away warm feelings are easy
Blanking out bad times
Is not too too difficult a task
It's not dealing with reality

It's living in the past
But I do want to say
Some things for clarity
Things past you that I'd like to pass

My poetry and my reading
Gratitude to you for that and more
The list of introductions is endless
You've learnt me all and evermore

The paintings and the painting
The galleries and the exhibitions
You bought me pastels, paints and board
You showed me shade and depth without derision

You may think I already knew sculpture
True I had visited Leeds, to see serene old Mr Moore

But you opened up the vista
Showing you, opened up, opened up my view

Then there's education
I guess that's where we met
You sometimes unkindly scoffed at my methods
By example you led, standards to aspire to you set

On this last night, I'm writing this in Kos
The flights delayed, we're losing waste less days
Now I know, or think I do, what it was like for you
In your horror of Fuerteventura

I didn't know then what you were feeling
I had forgotten, become so rotten
I had forgotten
Forgotten how to ask

Joris-Karl Huysmans (1848-1907)

This is a strange old time to write
Gone well past midnight
Waiting for the early morning late night flight

There's drinks and smokes
And artichokes for the well at heel
For me the writing hours is how I steal

I've read Mr Bukowski
And the Hippocrates oath
They've both travelled well, truth to tell

But this new book I've bought, I was caught
By the slip notes and the cover
Huysmans' *'A Rebours'* boy that's something other

His worldly ways are leading me, kneading me
I'll start with Edgar Allen Poe, or Paul Verlaine
Then on to Flaubert and Baudelaire

Oh he's stolen my every picture
As he passed this way
Before he passed away

But Joris Karl Huysmans he has not gone
No not gone
Only gone and put me in the clear

Mighty Mosquito

Drinking Water
Smoking Cigarettes
Chasing midges, forsaking rest
Camel cigarettes
Subtle flavour
Packed in blue

Pesky, pesky midges
Mosquito's cousins I guess
Here's hoping, hoping I'm choking them to death
Because they've had three meals or more
They've caught me unawares
Teetotal non-smoker, the one, it is 'he who dares'

The antisan cream
The disinfectants
Even the Germolene
Plus this net of finest denier
This nylon stocking sheen
Simply inept answers to the awesome biting machine

So I've snapped it
Between the pages of this here book
A fitting death
I hope you will think
A fitting, close fitting death
He died in a single scratch of ink.

Presented unwound and bound

I've saved the last words for you my girl
Before I set off home
You've been good company for me this week
Helped me through this time, real swell

Should you ever see this distant reflection
Should you ever browse this small collection
Presented for all, unwound and bound
I hope you have some satisfaction with your reaction

Who knows where the futures taking
Who knows where the past has gone
Who knows how love is answered
Who knows, who knows why we sing along

I'm gone

Sensual scenery

How long we've been
Been being cruel

How long we've starved ourselves
Of love's burning fuel

How many wasted opportunities
To enjoy each others sensual sceneries

Your sweet voice turned increasingly sour
I hesitated more and more, by each and every hour

Winking twinkling

Trinkets trickling, sprinkling
Winking twinkling

Fascinated by:
Imaginary days
Supersonic rays
Polished teak inlays
Roads to Mandalay
Sunlight through the maize

Winkles, twinkle toes
Sprinkle, tinkle trinkets

Captivated by:
Golden rose
Clothes to pose
Cerebral cerebrovascular
Vernacular
Spatial spectacular
Sunlight through the days

Spiv's and drones

Spiv's and drones
And semitones

Baronets and earls
Nylons for the girls

Spiv's and drones
Baronets and semitones

Communists and squatters
Prefabs for the potters

Spiv's and drones
Communists and semitones

Veterans and conscripts
Vouchers for the tit bits

Spiv's and drones
Veterans and semitones

Wobble

Wobbly
Strong cigarettes
Extremely cold water
Stiff, stiff drink
Touching your hand
Trembling
In sinking sand
Wobbly
One last time

No late night conversation

I don't know what your idea of friendship means
I don't know if being your best friend is what it seems
So I'll try and dissect your words
Through my mind, if remembered they may reverb

You don't want anything to do with being a couple
That solid statement's forward, that's not too subtle
You thought about counselling, decided too tired
You worked through options, except the lad I sired

You want for him to have a full parenting picture
You think it's weak, not strong, to let me, let him be
You say; If we don't have some contact with our boy
We'll lose what matters, and then there'll be no joy

So what does it mean exactly; best friend status
Do we progress, or second-guess our own hiatus
I felt clearer, although the cost was dearer
When we parted, not started, getting nearer

I can live with the parting glimpses of anger
Recollecting and putting blame, lapsing into languor
I think it is best, to not, not vocalise my thoughts
They may be off beam, for I am, I am out of sorts

Yet I don't want to look forward, too many days away
Thinking friendship means love, with a body sway
I don't want to waste any more years thinking it's OK
No real understanding, not to understand as we say

When clearly it's not so, for instance do you know
How you intend to befriend, or turn to love or no

If we don't find out shortly, no use to pretend
Our loving, our friendship will both come to an end

No cards, no notes no late night conversation
It's a funny kind of friendship without communication
There is no time left anywhere for making love
We do things that lovers aren't ever dreamt to do

Feel sand through fingers flowing

Sandals, stepping softly; impressions on the land
Seashells, washing softly; crustaceans in the sand
Lovers, walking softly; footsteps of the brand

Brass bands, jazz quartets; Shakespeare's in the park
Wind sail, skateboard trail; winter's dunes and dales
Sands, parks, love after dark; hands held at sunrise

Emotions
Seeping softly
Emotions
Feel sand through fingers flowing
Emotions flowing to the land

Memories
Keeping softly
Memories
Feel to command, sparkle glints glowing,
Memories glowing bright and grand

Strangers
Parting softly
Strangers
Feel sand, washed up
Strangers, washed up by the brand

Sandals, leaving softly; depressions on the land
Seashells, crushing; crusted crustaceans stand
Lovers talk not softly, lover's step's unplanned

Brass lands, of ports and quartz
Shakespeare's sister, blisters in the dark

Wind hail, broken rail; winter's tale, of time and pail
Slander, snark, smothered by dark, hands open to fail

Consigned to cognitive psychology

Staring out over, over waves for to wander
No turning back, nowhere is the space behind
Closed eyes, unable to close the subconscious
Staring out over sleep's depraved unconscious
Evading sleep, risks run to keep
Creep to keep, to keep a clear conscience
Consigned, resigned to cognitive psychology
Theory, practice, hypothesis, group therapy
Mind my mythology
Staring out over, over waves
Over waves for to ponder, longer

Consigned to reflective sociology

Brickyard stacks, fired by old coal slack
Cracks for through to wander
Chimneyed yards, prison guards, no turning back
Closed doors, wardens to close the conscience
Over out over the courtyard, marching unconscious
Prepare to sleep, to keep reaping their subconscious
Consigned, resigned to reflective sociology
Rote, rote together rote, rote on into my mythology
Stealing out over the exercise yard
Escape routes for to ponder longer

Arnold

Arnold
Pen strokes awake to smoke drifting far away
Smoke over mountain passes
Staining plains bought with molasses
Awake to stoke the boilers for to cruise

Arnold
Losing skilful classes, evening study, lads and lasses
Turning thoughts from study days to discotheques
Biblioteques for the masses
Clues that cruise among the shuffling stiletto shoes

Arnold
Choosing or being chosen
Stealing or being broken
Your words are my words spoken
Your solitudes are the lines I've chosen

Arnold
Opening and closing, in between a depth of reason
A season writing without love or muse to guide you
Ships across continents, sun and moon survive you
Choke, poke the cinders; one last fire, beside you

Arnold
Before the dark side, over away an swoon
Centuries apart, loves lost lying lonesome
Walking some solitary path from madness
Crazy diamond, life giving island, reflected moon

Stranded for the summer

An island in the summer
Sons of summer's sun
A beach, way down from my land

Down for the summer
An island in the summer
Your island's downs, astound throughout the summer

Your island, save for your son
It is your summer's summer
You're my island, you are my island for the summer

My island is yours, our island for the summer
Sand washed, sun dyed
Dried out island for the summer

Bleach blonde, beach bombs
Plundered the summer's summer
Blonde on blonde, beach bombs

Blondes for your summer
Your blonde beach bombs
Blondes play on

Through the summer's summer
Oh my our sweet not sour, island summer
Sun dried, bleach dyed, blonde eyes

Crying out for the summer
Blondes lied, beaches tried, tied up for the summer
Tie dyed, bleary eyed

Plied up, belied for the summer
Island wide, eyelids slide
Cried up for the summer

Turning tides, island rides
All supplied, all are up for the summer
Ride away, we planned to stay

Stray away, for the summer
Dreams stranded on the sand
Stranded for another summer

Setting simple preparations

Distraction; rise early in the morning
Without outward conversation
Conversing in silence, in prayer
Minds in a meditative clean slate state
Washed by our own meandering
Centred, entering nothingness, not loss

Making space for some other, another's message
Making space for some other, another's invitation
Making space and ambiance to surround you
Clear mind for to think, think clear thoughts through
Think without sinking down to the inner depths
Or climbing false escalations, or wieldy expectations
Setting simple preparations

To raise a tide on an even keel
Not stealing another's visualisations
Except for some that share the cross
But it does't need to be religions
And it does not necessarily mean faith
What it is that I am after
Is not to be led, not led nor fed, by distraction

To derive salvation, discovering inner satisfaction
From doubt without to an inner clarity of vision
A lucidity returning, thoughts thought that I'd lost
Brooding for another's group I'm now removing
Wood shedding this blessing I'm smoothly grooving
How, you know, watch me let my best friend grow
How, let my friend remember, let go, for to grow

Rothko at the Tate

Maroon and Grey
Meditation Way
Babes to Stay
Tantric Play

Destruction disruption

Vesuvius
Molten rocks
For swollen scars
Eruptions
Disruptions for woken souls

Madagascar
Fallen stocks
For open stars
Corruptions
Disruptions for spoken calls

Ayres rock
Risen shock
For shaman shahs
Expulsions
Disruptions for fallen walls

With gravitas, love, love, love

This poem should be read slowly
Slowly
More slowly now
Slow real down
For this single word
Surreal slow
Slow now
With gravitas
And concentration
Pursed lips
Rasping throat
Breathe
Breathe again
Again breathe
Settle
Oxygenate the root canal
Feel the solar plexus
Begin to give birth
Give birth
Birth to a word
A word from the tomb of time
Relax, oh Frankie, relax
Obliterate all your other thoughts
Clear space, no space, anyplace
Slowly
Slow
Down low
Low
With gravitas
Conscious of the consequence
Memories of resonance
Give

Give birth
Birth to love
Love
Love, love, love
Love

Music of the spheres

Sphere
Lyrical
Satirical
Sphere
Political

Lyrical
Satirical
Sphere
Whimsical

Satirical
Sphere
Whimsical

Sphere
Miracle

Physical

No need to laugh

Pictures, paintings and photographs
Still life, portrait, landscape and pornograph
Quiet, loud, stone deaf, no need to laugh
Canvas, razor blade, splash, slash the gaff
Riff-raff, taffy and terry, top floor, up the caff

Prescribe instead

No need to verbalise
Just no need
Feel the faith
Hold it for yourself

Feel free
No need to describe
Or feel trapped
Without words to share

Stare in to your own blank space
Safe from prying eyes
Clear the need
Critics of your description

Prescribe instead
Wider read, journey's wed
Sun steps to moon steps
Coronets to coronations

Within the abbey
Within
Feel the faith
Hold it for yourself

Your faith
Yours only

Vanishing under varnish

Lillie pond
Eyes wide open
Petals laying
On water swaying
Stems proud
Slice the shining surface
Wandering by
Caught the eye
Canvas
Vanishing under varnish
Tarnished impression
Suggestion liaisons
Woken
Eyes wide open
And seeing
And being
Seeing movement
Being moved
Moved by petals
Petals laying
On water swaying

Slight craves

Ah
Clear thought

White waves
Blue sky

Message in a bottle

Hip
Twist top

Slight craves
Addicts lie

Message in a bottle

Don't get angry, don't get even

Don't get angry
Don't get even
Don't get down

Try to fly

No

Wait on

Work through anger
Work towards even
Build up from down

Now you'll fly

The wonder of rebuff dismissed

You want to communicate
That is you want to say something
To cause some reactions

You want to communicate a closing
That is you want to say something
To close words of birth contractions

Now then here is the dilemma
By saying nothing
Do you communicate more than words can ever say

Or
By saying nothing
Do you precursor, and so prevent reaction

If your words are spoken
Can the meaning be more mistaken
Than if the written word was read

If your words are laid on parchment paper
Is spontaneity lost
The wonder of rebuff dismissed

Redirection distressed, pointed out by no one other
Do you have the craft or guile
With words to smile or cry

Or look through sly eyes wily
With style to climb on high
While still saying, swaying, saying nigh

Shuffle the raffle

Like a sparrows wing you were broken
Whilst I was feasting on Baudelaire
Hustle, harrow among dust bowls, soft words spoken
Never near, once more we, we were keeping clear

Midnight hour, crescent moon, for you the only token
Whilst I immersed in Poe and Mr. Arnold dear
Shuffle, ruffle, audits amongst dawn's chorus woken
Ever to steer, rudder less throughout the sphere

Autograph your dicrotic cast

That rook and that fair raven
Over the sea from Milford Haven
Cigarettes stamped 'A' by company Craven

Ashberry and yew, and years spent misbehaving
Words untrue, lines that slew, croons that keep on slaving
Crows and crows and thought yo yo's, leaving and waving

The hour glass tipped and turned to yesterday
The wayward path tripped to Everglade
The Sunshine orchestra is ready for the stage

That rook and that fair raven
Grass and dales, pail with ships that sailed
Rails into the distance on cowpokes trails

Leaves of glass on shattered brass
Diamonds; the impasse from rusty pasts
Lust and laugh, autograph your dicrotic cast

Sunk, I've fallen out of love

My demented mind descended
Pretended it had been doing good

My times past have been lamented
Cemented dams opened to the flood

All past promises are now rescinded
Crescendo to the sound of going rough

Your likes, dislikes, flights of fancy are contended
They are sent packing, with the candle that I snuff

No more string-less invitations extended
One too many open arms, becalm unfriendly stuff

Happy times stored safe, easily remembered
You have cut me so so deep with your indifference

So deep
I am sunk, and so I have fallen out of love

Ken

Then it's a new life, ken
Stride for, from strife, to strike, to ken
Blow away the smokescreen, ken
A new day, a new persona, do you ken

Stir it up

Stir it up
Don't stir it up
Again

Trip up
Tripped up
Once before

Slip cup
Slip of satin silk
Skip

Strap
Fond shoulder
Trap

Yes, that glitterati literati stuff

Lavender swing and Russian vine
Boy it spreads like swine
That Prussian wine

Garden gate and summer fete
Boy isn't England great
At that washing plate

Shower and brush, I'm coming up lush
Oh that teenage crush
Rash it up, listen for thong and thrush

Library books and surfers touch
Yes, that glitterati literati stuff
Ledbury's found, all bound and butch

Jazz and soul and rock and roll
Dwell upon that digital ball
Soak up that frock, astride your cockle stall

Dreamy lair

Your essence waved, my wafted air
I'd taken time and crafted, serenity to share
Then the blue sky turned to gold

Your effervescence duly staffed, my dreamy lair
I waited less than wandered, in incandescent prayer
Then the clouds, lined with silver, softly rolled

Your presence presents, a trembling bare
I'd opened, once again, this strange affair
Then the red moon rose, by the setting sun

Your lessons in love, lent in a gentle stare
I'd been carefree, lest care made me beware
Then the sky opened all the way to heaven

Your defence, immense at first, wavered there
I'd shown relentless perseverance, a scattered flare
Then you said take my hand our thighs to fondle

We wandered amongst the wonder stuff
We wondered, how we would share
Then the night turned, scared, into a dull grey day

The devil levels

Decorating cakes and winning medals
Elephants up the stairs push bike pedals
Crushing dust brushing up the pebbles
Footprints on hot coals as the devil levels
Expecting wakes thirst slaking revellers
Bedevilled brakes Turin meddles dwell

A last goodbye

Hands upon my shoulder
Clasp before you cry
Warmth flowing
Parting
A last goodbye

Hands around the waistline
Clench touch you try
Warmth flowing
Parting
A last goodbye

Hands stroke the neck nape
Massage nervous lobes you pry
Warmth flowing
Parting
Goodbye

These are only words

Wherever you are now
Whatever your circumstance
Reading my words
You only have from me my words

This sound I hear
This inclination dear
Into ether disappears
Into only my words

I could try to pace
Run then such a race
This space embrace
But still you only have my words

I could remind you of a picture
Dedicate colours richer
Embroider with stitch and pitcher
Only for you to only have my words

Recreate a journey
Pray up to eternity
Praise gods gift maternity
But still you only have my words

Seems your help is needed
Your adoption and adaptation pleaded
Between the lines re-seeded
Making more than only my words

Turn this into meditation
Find your cross, fix your station

Deliver to your inner nation
Staying, saying only with my words

Slow down now
Introduce your own sounds around
Hear that distant bell
Foretell your shell around my words

Slow down again
Listen to the raindrops
Splash your playful puddles
Wash your water over my words

Slow down to a whisper
Kiss the touch that missed her
Remember your mother, your sister
Bring your family into my words

Now you are calm and serene
Feeling goodness in between
Your soul and body clean
Sheen your sparkle on my words

Tomorrow we'll do the jazz
The rock and the razzamatazz
Nights out with the lads
Blast my words loud into the night

We'll pour the wine and whisky
Move up close, get frisky
Forget who takes the biscuit
Recall my illicit words

In front of the magistrate with remorse

Your honour, sorry; of course, of course
We were pretending, like the bourse
Reciting only my words

In prison cell and courtyard
Dwelling on what is, and what might have been
You thought it was the truth you'd seen
But it was only only my words

Back at the beginning
A chorus chord for singing
In your ears you can hear them ringing
These are only my words

Burning no delphinium

That's thinned it down to jealousy
For one to someone's daughters husband
For another an old colleague or school governor
Perhaps some artistic friends at theatre
There might even have been someone's brothers
Though not my neighbour, the father of our dreams
Your words never led me, said to me to think him so

Then really it's about possession
This crazy daft obsession
Don't ever learn the lesson
The crescent moon turns sharp too soon
As we cut the cloth with silence
Men of words condemned by hesitance
Blown away and up in smoke by reticence

It's a madness bordering delirium
Scrawling this elemental prescription cerium
For you to read it's more than tedium
Extremis no grounds for seeking medium
Crazed and senseless past remedium
One more cigarette growing no delphinium
A glass of milk and back along the continuum

Pretty words and parting flowers

Then I rationalise it as jealousy
Making sense with no sense
There was I'm quite certain, there was a shaky feeling

I have been misled, for certain, or were you dealing
Pretty words and parting flowers
Remembering the movies, remembering *'The Hours'*

When the balance began, began by getting lost
The red mist, angers languor, senseless loss
I sensed loss at any cost

Driving at midnight, up country over a fault free line
Up country; simmer's settle, thought process fettled
The madness mellows, wallows in the moonshine

Gave, given

I gave up all I had
I almost gave up alcohol
I gave up friends and family
I almost gave up rock and roll

I gave up any expectation
I almost gave up sexual strolls
I gave up dare and doing
I almost gave up blues and soul

I gave up thought and conversation
I almost gave up waves that rise and fall
I gave up more than this and all
The day my love you stole

You have given up on friendly pretending
You almost had me sold
You have given up on futures intending
You almost turned me cold

You have given up on dreams extending
You almost cast me in your mould
You have given up on pleasures lending
You almost dried my love juice, up there in the fold

You have given up on letters sending
You almost stole the words I've scrawled
You have given up more than this and all
The day our love wasted, haste turned new to old

Read by Delacroix

But you got no reaction
Not a single missing beat
In fact the breath was less
Less than a distant tantric bless

So it's time to stop the reason
The seasons past and full
Her emotions have been gathered
Gathered up for the cull

The breath was not held
Ever less and seldom welled
The conversation was lukewarm
Lukewarm going on dull

And in between the spaces
Where once lay hope and joy
Now, there, in between the spaces
Lies less hope than read by Delacroix

Can this break the bond that binds and blinds
The empty sound to shatter, splatter scattered minds
Silent chords to carve, to cut some umbilical heave
Deceive time wasted, receive tasted hope to believe

Aspiring Form

Aspiring form
Magic numbers
I could not find a rhyme
I searched my mind
And stumbled upon a rumba
Or was it a rhombus parallelogram

An imaginary rabbit
Occurred through some simulation
The magic words
I'd heard
It caught my imagination
Misfired
I'd aspired once again to slumber

Cusp of Sea

Cobalt blue, cusp of sea
Remember
Remember
Remember me

Wave tops, roll mops
Rescue
Rescue
Rescue me

Lapping, waves clapping

Ripples in the sand
Ageless land, ageless land
Fishing man and weaving hands
Ageless, ageless land

Motor boats and seagull croaks
Cappuccino with cakes to soak
Motor boats and wheels of hope
Ageless, timeless land

Lapping, waves clapping
Splashing in the sea
A pink champagne bikini
A splash of cloth, my ageless mind receding

Plumb, aplomb, and sweet bon-bon

Lunch today
Was rocket and rye
Try if I might I could not buy
Salami and fries

We're an international audience
The figs didn't stand a chance
The square rigger sailed, wind full on
Plumb, aplomb, and sweet bon-bon

Wild ocean, sea spray
Dive bomber
What's that between your teeth
Wild ocean's barrier reef

Cormorant and cockatiel
Peking duck for three
Old grey seal, who do you feel
Across the splashing sea

Safe shores in between

Deep, deep ocean
Deep black, deep blue, deep green
Deep, deep ocean
Samurai and Viking and safe shores in between

Was it a mirage
Or a marriage
Were you married
To the sea

Single form

Single form
Dormitory norm
Fags in all the pictures
You chiselled stone
Made broken homes
Sculpture's first lady

Your workshop
And your garden
For wearers of Elizabeth Arden
As become
In summer sun
An annual communication

To exercise with a moulder's touch
Your work was such
Drawing friends of sculpture
Their dreams to clutch
Yorkshire girl, your strings and swirls
You've captivated with such wonder

Higher ground

I came to catch the light of summer
I came from higher ground
I caught the cape in early summer
I caught the sunlight, going down

This is Sennen Cove

It is June the 22nd
The sky is blue
The sea is green
This is
Sennen Cove

A coffee cup
A cigarette
A pretty girl walks by
Erotic glands exotic plants
This is Sennen Cove

Whites and blues
Sun gold hues
Atlantic muse
It's all good news
This is Sennen Cove

Surfboard suits
Diving boots
De la mer fruits
Dolphin loops
This is Sennen Cove

On the beach at Sennen

Sennen
Oh Sennen
Imagine
Mr. Lennon
On the beach
At Sennen

Or even Mr. Rea
Words to disappear
Driving home for Christmas
Driving on to Sennen
Seven stairways to heaven
On the beach at Sennen

June, July or December
In passing times remember
That god's earth let you lend her
Returned once more to send her
Spend your lent
Heaven sent
On the beach at Sennen

It is as if the ever after

On the beach at Sennen
As close on earth to heaven
Sunlight smiles and laughter
It is as if the ever after

Breeze blue jay

Carbis Bay
Fortunes far away
A place to stay
For rejuvenation

Midsummer's day
Breeze blue jay
Walk and play
For recuperation

Crimson skin of Lincoln

Granite Boulder
Strapless shoulder
Ultramarine
Are you

Mother of pearl
Countess, King and Earl
Carbon blue it's true
You're diamond through and through

Crimson skin of Lincoln
Your friends to whom you think on
Though only the amethyst knew
Who or why the seagull slew

Moving swift

The Nokia is new
I'm driving through
I'm leaving for no reason

The Lexus boy
Air conditioned joy
Feels like I am committing treason

Through this place called Drift
Moving swift, through the gears I shift
I'm all for going out of season

Not a pixel richer

Doing the Japanese
No time to please
Just point and click
And move on quick

Megabytes of memory
Seminar and plenary
Twenty first third century
Moving on past sensory

Cease the moment
Not the picture
Photographic truth
Not a pixel richer

Or what to trot out

Time to dwell
My words to tell
Caught in the spell
Of lines that rhyme

Or don't
Or won't

Pubic roots
And pheasant shoots
You can see
To where my mind is sinking

Or can't
Or shan't

Baby belle
And pelvic swell
It's lust not love
I'm drinking

Or what
To trot out

Celtic summer frocks

I'll think of her more than I can thank her
My minds been like a canker
I've walked along the waters edge
I've trod my footsteps in the sand to pledge

So stay awhile
Beneath this summer smile
Observe these soaring cliffs
Beneath of which I sit to sift

Soliloquy or fast
Passed places ever last
Moss and luxurious lichen
Waters from the kitchen

Its fibered growth turns grumbling rocks
In to the colours of Celtic summer frocks
Sand, and sand, through twisted toes does tumble
Grains to maintain this odd refrain so humble

Again sustained by summer's sun
Upon which I sure must not stumble

Endless stew

Its been four months of poems
Since she asked me to be going

That's long enough for other stuff
To take me off and trawling

So what stops you lad, what drives you mad
What holds you back, from your oats a sowing

Well if that I knew, in this endless stew
I would have ended by forgoing

Inclinations

Endless complications
Wordless conversations
Forgotten combinations
Splendid isolations

Removed from all temptations
Distance dulled sensations
No communiqué or revelations
Dependant isolations

Craving recreations
Return on base to stations
A pairing of incantations
A wasted life of separations

Crampons for security

You're galvanised with energy
I'm corroding, turning rust to dust

Your stainless sheen is shining
My pitted mind is blind

You're climbing cliff-tops surely
I'm using crampons for security

Your certainty is widening
Yourself you're swiftly finding

My broken shafts are not for laughs
These words, they're just the gas

Enjoy the fruits of summer

Avocado prawn
Avogadro's norm
Enjoy the fruits of summer

Forget the beef and grizzle
And the turkey twizzle
Instead pray let the herb oils drizzle

It's more than just a breeze

We're dealing with the wonderment
It's more than just a breeze
This rock face is shorn
By the waves of scorn
It's more than just a breeze

That last cigarette, a simple bet
It's more than just a breeze
This habit worn
For years forlorn
It's more than just a wheeze

Down at Godrevy

Sea cold coca cola
Salt and Asti Spumante
Champagne supernova
Big blue Atlantic sea

There's burger and there's onions
There are barbecues for free
Away from mother Meavy
Down at Godrevy

There's mother's flying kites
With ladders in their tights
Its natures might
This big blue Atlantic Sea

Sun's been up for hours
Though it's the going down I've come to see
I'm captured by the guileless wonder
Of Godrevy's big blue Atlantic sea

Printed in Poland
by Amazon Fulfillment
Poland Sp. z o.o., Wrocław

55547543R00127